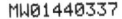

CONTENTS

Understanding the MAP Tests 3

Purpose and Benefits of MAP Testing 4

Test Format and Content.. 4

Adaptive Testing and Scoring System 5

Preparing for Success on the MAP Test... 5

What Is Contained Within this Book? 6

Topic 1 – Capitalization... 7

Topic 1 - Answers 17

Topic 2 – Punctuation 19

Topic 2 - Answers 29

Topic 3 – Pronouns... 31

Topic 3 - Answers 41

Topic 4 – Adjectives 43

Topic 4 - Answers 53

Topic 5 – Word Meaning 55
Topic 5 - Answers 65
Topic 6 – Nouns 67
Topic 6 - Answers 77
Topic 7 – Tenses 79
Topic 7 – Answers 89
Topic 8 – Prepositions 91
Topic 8 – Answers 101
Ready for More? 103

Understanding the MAP Tests

The NWEA MAP (Measures of Academic Progress) test is an adaptive assessment that is designed to measure student growth and progress in a variety of subject areas. The test is taken by millions of students across the United States and is widely used by educators to help inform instruction and measure student outcomes. The NWEA MAP test is administered online and provides immediate feedback on student performance, allowing teachers to adjust their teaching strategies and provide targeted support to individual students.

The NWEA MAP test is unique in that it is adaptive, which means that the difficulty of the questions adjusts based on the student's responses. This allows the test to be more personalized to each student's abilities and provides a more accurate measure of their knowledge and skills. The test covers a range of subject areas, including mathematics, reading, language usage, and science, and is administered multiple times throughout the school year. This allows teachers to track student progress and growth over time and make data-driven decisions to improve student outcomes.

Purpose and Benefits of MAP Testing

The primary purpose of the MAP Test is to provide valuable insights into a student's learning and academic progress. By offering a detailed analysis of a student's performance in reading, language usage, mathematics, and science, the test helps teachers tailor their instruction to meet individual needs. The MAP Test also serves as a benchmarking tool, allowing schools and districts to compare their students' performance with national norms and other local institutions.

This data-driven approach enables educators to make informed decisions about curriculum, instructional methods, and resource allocation, ultimately leading to improved student outcomes. Additionally, the MAP Test can help identify gifted students who may benefit from advanced or accelerated programs, as well as students who may require additional support or interventions.

Test Format and Content

The MAP Test is divided into four primary content areas: reading, language usage, mathematics, and science. Each section consists of multiple-choice questions that cover various topics and skills within the respective subject. The test is untimed, allowing students to work at their own pace and ensuring a lower level of test anxiety. The computer-adaptive nature of the MAP Test ensures that the difficulty of questions adjusts based on a student's performance, making it suitable for students of all ability levels. As a result, the MAP Test not only evaluates a student's mastery of grade-level content but also assesses their readiness for more advanced material.

Adaptive Testing and Scoring System

One of the unique aspects of the MAP Test is its adaptive testing system. As students answer questions, the test adjusts the difficulty of subsequent questions based on their performance. This adaptive nature allows the test to home in on a student's true ability level, providing more accurate and meaningful results. The MAP Test uses a RIT (Rasch Unit) scale to measure student achievement, which is an equal-interval scale that allows for easy comparison of scores across grade levels and subjects. This scoring system allows educators and parents to track a student's growth over time, making it an invaluable tool for understanding academic progress and setting individualized learning goals.

Preparing for Success on the MAP Test

Effective preparation for the MAP Test involves a combination of understanding the test format, mastering content knowledge, and developing test-taking strategies. This test prep book is designed to provide students with comprehensive guidance on each content area, offering targeted instruction and practice questions to build confidence and ensure success. Additionally, the book includes test-taking tips and strategies to help students approach the test with a calm and focused mindset. By working through this book and dedicating time to consistent practice, students will be well-equipped to excel on the MAP Test and achieve their academic goals.

Note that, since there is no cap to the level that a student can work to in preparation for this test, there is no 'completion' of content, as students can simply do questions from grades above in preparation. It should be noted that students are not expected to work far above grade level to succeed in this test, as consistent correct answers are more relevant.

What Is Contained Within this Book?

Within this book you will find 320 questions based off content which would be found within the MAP test your student will take. The content found in this book will be the equivalent of grade 1 level. Note that since this test is adaptive, some students may benefit by looking at several grade levels of content, not just their own.

At the end of the book will contain answers alongside explanations. It is recommended to look and check your answers thoroughly in regular intervals to make sure you improve as similar questions come up.

Number	Topic Name	Questions	Answers
1	Capitalization	p7	p17
2	Punctuation	P19	P29
3	Pronouns	P31	P41
4	Adjectives	P43	P53
5	Word Meaning	P55	P65
6	Nouns	P67	P77
7	Tenses	P79	P89
8	Prepositions	P91	P101

Topic 1 – Capitalization

1.1) Which word needs a capital letter?

☐ dog

☐ run

☐ tree

☐ monday

1.2) Which word needs a capital letter?

☐ jump

☐ june

☐ car

☐ ball

1.3) Which word needs a capital letter?

☐ cat

☐ play

☐ sara

☐ book

1.4) Which word needs a capital letter?

☐ mouse

☐ america

☐ shoe

☐ eat

1.5) Which word needs a capital letter?

☐ sing

☐ january

☐ plant

☐ horse

1.6) Which word needs a capital letter?

☐ bob

☐ run

☐ fish

☐ pencil

1.7) Which word needs a capital letter?

☐ tree

☐ london

☐ frog

☐ read

1.8) Which word needs a capital letter?

☐ december

☐ snake

☐ chair

☐ dance

1.9) Which word needs a capital letter?

☐ bird

☐ sleep

☐ george

☐ table

1.10) Which word needs a capital letter?

☐ bag

☐ cow

☐ swim

☐ friday

1.11) Which word should start with a capital letter?

☐ school

☐ june

☐ ball

☐ dog

1.12) Which word is the name of a month?

☐ play

☐ december

☐ run

☐ cat

1.13) What is the correct way to write the first word in a sentence?

☐ cat

☐ The

☐ jumped

☐ over

1.14) Which name needs a capital letter?

☐ alice

☐ ball

☐ sing

☐ eat

1.15) Which word should be capitalized?

☐ january

☐ plant

☐ car

☐ horse

1.16) What is the capital letter for the word 'paris'?

☐ p

☐ a

☐ r

☐ i

1.17) Find the proper noun in the list.

☐ table

☐ george

☐ bird

☐ sleep

1.18) What is the capital letter for the word 'tuesday'?

☐ s

☐ u

☐ e

☐ t

1.19) Which word is a proper noun?

☐ london

☐ read

☐ tree

☐ frog

1.20) Which one is the name of a person?

☐ mouse

☐ bob

☐ eat

☐ shoe

1.21) Which word needs a capital letter?

☐ tuesday

☐ dog

☐ run

☐ ball

1.22) Which is the name of a country?

☐ canada

☐ ball

☐ book

☐ run

1.23) Choose the word that should be capitalized.

☐ october

☐ plant

☐ car

☐ jump

1.24) Which word is a name?

☐ susan

☐ book

☐ car

☐ eat

1.25) What is the first word of a sentence?

☐ dog

☐ shoe

☐ plant

☐ Today

1.26) Select the day of the week.

☐ run

☐ monday

☐ frog

☐ ball

1.27) Which word needs to be capitalized?

☐ bird

☐ read

☐ september

☐ cat

1.28) Which of these is a city?

☐ car

☐ jump

☐ paris

☐ tree

1.29) Which word needs a capital letter?

☐ run

☐ dog

☐ eat

☐ march

1.30) Choose the word that is the name of a person.

☐ plant

☐ sing

☐ ball

☐ john

1.31) Which word should be capitalized?

☐ april

☐ sing

☐ car

☐ frog

1.32) Which is the name of a person?

☐ lisa

☐ ball

☐ jump

☐ cat

1.33) Choose the word that needs a capital letter.

☐ new york

☐ dog

☐ read

☐ plant

1.34) Select the proper noun.

☐ shoe

☐ michael

☐ car

☐ eat

1.35) Which word is a month?

☐ run

☐ frog

☐ book

☐ november

1.36) Which needs to be capitalized?

☐ plant

☐ dog

☐ car

☐ friday

1.37) Which word is the name of a city?

☐ bird

☐ cat

☐ jump

☐ london

1.38) What is the correct way to write the first word in a sentence?

☐ She

☐ plant

☐ shoe

☐ dog

1.39) Select the word that should be capitalized.

☐ car

☐ saturday

☐ read

☐ frog

1.40) Which word needs a capital letter?

☐ jump

☐ ball

☐ december

☐ cat

Topic 1 - Answers

Question Number	Answer	Explanation
1.1	monday	Days of the week are proper nouns and need capitalization.
1.2	june	Names of months are proper nouns and need capitalization.
1.3	sara	Proper names need capitalization.
1.4	america	Names of countries are proper nouns and need capitalization.
1.5	january	Names of months are proper nouns and need capitalization.
1.6	bob	Proper names need capitalization.
1.7	london	Names of cities are proper nouns and need capitalization.
1.8	december	Names of months are proper nouns and need capitalization.
1.9	george	Proper names need capitalization.
1.10	friday	Days of the week are proper nouns and need capitalization.
1.11	june	Names of months are proper nouns and need capitalization.
1.12	december	Names of months are proper nouns and need capitalization.
1.13	The	The first word in a sentence should start with a capital letter.
1.14	alice	Proper names need capitalization.
1.15	january	Names of months are proper nouns and need capitalization.
1.16	p	The word 'paris' is a proper noun and should be capitalized as 'Paris'.
1.17	george	Proper nouns like 'George' need capitalization.
1.18	t	The word 'tuesday' is a proper noun and should be capitalized as 'Tuesday'.

1.19	london	Names of cities are proper nouns and need capitalization.
1.20	bob	Proper names need capitalization.
1.21	tuesday	Days of the week are proper nouns and need capitalization.
1.22	canada	Names of countries are proper nouns and need capitalization.
1.23	october	Names of months are proper nouns and need capitalization.
1.24	susan	Proper names need capitalization.
1.25	Today	The first word in a sentence should start with a capital letter.
1.26	monday	Days of the week are proper nouns and need capitalization.
1.27	september	Names of months are proper nouns and need capitalization.
1.28	paris	Names of cities are proper nouns and need capitalization.
1.29	march	Names of months are proper nouns and need capitalization.
1.30	john	Proper names need capitalization.
1.31	april	Names of months are proper nouns and need capitalization.
1.32	lisa	Proper names need capitalization.
1.33	new york	Names of cities are proper nouns and need capitalization.
1.34	michael	Proper names need capitalization.
1.35	november	Names of months are proper nouns and need capitalization.
1.36	friday	Days of the week are proper nouns and need capitalization.
1.37	london	Names of cities are proper nouns and need capitalization.
1.38	She	The first word in a sentence should start with a capital letter.
1.39	saturday	Days of the week are proper nouns and need capitalization.
1.40	december	Names of months are proper nouns and need capitalization.

Topic 2 - Punctuation

2.1) Which sentence is correct?

☐ The dog runs.

☐ the dog runs

☐ The dog runs

☐ the dog runs?

2.2) What punctuation mark ends a question?

☐ !

☐ ?

☐ ,

☐ .

2.3) Choose the correct sentence.

☐ Where is the cat

☐ Where is the cat?

☐ where is the cat?

☐ where is the cat

2.4) Which sentence has a period?

☐ I like to play!

☐ I like to play?

☐ i like to play.

☐ I like to play

2.5) Which sentence is correct?

☐ She is happy.

☐ She is happy?

☐ she is happy

☐ she is happy.

2.6) What punctuation mark ends a statement?

☐ ,

☐ ?

☐ .

☐ !

2.7) Choose the correct sentence.

☐ can you help me

☐ Can you help me?

☐ can you help me?

☐ Can you help me

2.8) Which sentence has a question mark?

☐ Are you coming!

☐ Are you coming.

☐ are you coming?

☐ Are you coming

2.9) Which sentence is correct?

☐ He likes to jump!

☐ he likes to jump

☐ he likes to jump.

☐ He likes to jump.

2.10) What punctuation mark ends an exclamation?

☐ .

☐ ?

☐ !

☐ ,

2.11) Choose the sentence with the correct punctuation.

☐ It is sunny today.

☐ It is sunny today

☐ It is sunny today?

☐ It is sunny today!

2.12) Which sentence has a question mark?

☐ Is it time to go

☐ is it time to go?

☐ Is it time to go!

☐ Is it time to go.

2.13) What punctuation mark does not end a sentence?

- .
- ,
- ?
- !

2.14) Which sentence is correct?

- we are going home.
- We are going home.
- we are going home
- We are going home!

2.15) Choose the correct sentence.

- Why is it raining
- why is it raining
- why is it raining?
- Why is it raining?

2.16) Which sentence needs to add a period?

- I have a book?
- I have a book!
- i have a book.
- I have a book

2.17) What punctuation mark do we use for excitement?

- [ ] .
- [ ] ?
- [ ] ,
- [ ] !

2.18) Which sentence is correct?

- [ ] They are playing.
- [ ] They are playing
- [ ] they are playing.
- [ ] they are playing

2.19) Choose the correct punctuation for a question.

- [ ] .
- [ ] ,
- [ ] ?
- [ ] !

2.20) Which sentence needs to add an exclamation mark?

- [ ] Wow, that is amazing
- [ ] Wow, that is amazing.
- [ ] Wow, that is amazing?
- [ ] wow, that is amazing!

2.21) Which sentence needs to add a period?

☐ She has a red ball?

☐ She has a red ball!

☐ She has a red ball

☐ she has a red ball.

2.22) Choose the sentence with the correct punctuation.

☐ The cat is sleeping

☐ The cat is sleeping?

☐ The cat is sleeping!

☐ The cat is sleeping.

2.23) What punctuation mark ends a statement?

☐ ,

☐ !

☐ .

☐ ?

2.24) Which sentence is correct?

☐ do you like apples

☐ do you like apples?

☐ Do you like apples?

☐ Do you like apples

2.25) Choose the correct punctuation for excitement.

☐ ,

☐ ?

☐ !

☐ .

2.26) Which sentence needs a question mark added?

☐ can we go now?

☐ Can we go now!

☐ Can we go now

☐ Can we go now.

2.27) What punctuation mark do we use for a question?

☐ .

☐ !

☐ ?

☐ ,

2.28) Which sentence is correct?

☐ She is very happy.

☐ she is very happy

☐ She is very happy?

☐ she is very happy.

2.29) Choose the sentence with the correct punctuation.

☐ how are you

☐ How are you

☐ how are you?

☐ How are you?

2.30) Which sentence has an exclamation mark?

☐ That is awesome?

☐ That is awesome

☐ that is awesome!

☐ That is awesome.

2.31) Which sentence needs a period added?

☐ We went to the park!

☐ We went to the park?

☐ we went to the park.

☐ We went to the park

2.32) Choose the sentence with the correct punctuation.

☐ He has a blue car

☐ He has a blue car?

☐ He has a blue car.

☐ He has a blue car!

2.33) What punctuation mark ends a excited statement?

☐ ?

☐ .

☐ !

☐ ,

2.34) Which sentence is correct?

☐ Please close the door.

☐ please close the door.

☐ please close the door

☐ Please close the door?

2.35) Choose the correct punctuation for a question.

☐ !

☐ ,

☐ ?

☐ .

2.36) Which sentence needs a period added?

☐ i like ice cream.

☐ I like ice cream

☐ I like ice cream!

☐ I like ice cream?

2.37) What punctuation mark do we use for excitement?

- ☐ .
- ☐ !
- ☐ ?
- ☐ ,

2.38) Which sentence is correct?

- ☐ can you see the stars?
- ☐ Can you see the stars?
- ☐ Can you see the stars
- ☐ can you see the stars

2.39) Choose the sentence with the correct punctuation.

- ☐ The dog is barking!
- ☐ The dog is barking?
- ☐ The dog is barking.
- ☐ The dog is barking

2.40) Which sentence needs an exclamation mark added?

- ☐ That is amazing
- ☐ that is amazing!
- ☐ That is amazing?
- ☐ That is amazing.

Topic 2 - Answers

Question Number	Answer	Explanation
2.1	The dog runs.	Correct capitalization and punctuation.
2.2	?	A question mark ends a question.
2.3	Where is the cat?	Correct punctuation for a question.
2.4	i like to play.	Correct punctuation for a statement.
2.5	She is happy.	Correct capitalization and punctuation.
2.6	.	A period ends a statement.
2.7	Can you help me?	Correct capitalization and punctuation for a question.
2.8	are you coming?	Correct punctuation for a question.
2.9	He likes to jump.	Correct capitalization and punctuation.
2.10	!	An exclamation mark ends an exclamation.
2.11	It is sunny today.	Correct punctuation for a statement.
2.12	is it time to go?	Correct punctuation for a question.
2.13	,	A comma does not end a sentence.
2.14	We are going home.	Correct capitalization and punctuation.
2.15	Why is it raining?	Correct capitalization and punctuation for a question.
2.16	I have a book	Needs a period to end the statement.
2.17	!	An exclamation mark is used for excitement.
2.18	They are playing.	Correct capitalization and punctuation.
2.19	?	A question mark is used for a question.
2.20	Wow, that is amazing	Needs an exclamation mark for excitement.

2.21	She has a red ball	Needs a period to end the statement.
2.22	The cat is sleeping.	Correct punctuation for a statement.
2.23	.	A period ends a statement.
2.24	Do you like apples?	Correct capitalization and punctuation for a question.
2.25	!	An exclamation mark is used for excitement.
2.26	Can we go now	Needs a question mark for the question.
2.27	?	A question mark is used for a question.
2.28	She is very happy.	Correct capitalization and punctuation.
2.29	How are you?	Correct capitalization and punctuation for a question.
2.30	that is awesome!	Correct punctuation for excitement.
2.31	We went to the park	Needs a period to end the statement.
2.32	He has a blue car.	Correct punctuation for a statement.
2.33	!	An exclamation mark ends an excited statement.
2.34	Please close the door.	Correct capitalization and punctuation.
2.35	?	A question mark is used for a question.
2.36	I like ice cream	Needs a period to end the statement.
2.37	!	An exclamation mark is used for excitement.
2.38	Can you see the stars?	Correct capitalization and punctuation for a question.
2.39	The dog is barking!	Correct punctuation for excitement.
2.40	That is amazing	Needs an exclamation mark for excitement.

Topic 3 - Pronouns

3.1) Which word can replace 'Tom'?

☐ She

☐ It

☐ They

☐ He

3.2) Which word can replace 'Lisa'?

☐ He

☐ They

☐ She

☐ It

3.3) Which word can replace 'the cat'?

☐ She

☐ They

☐ He

☐ It

3.4) Which word can replace 'the boys'?

☐ They

☐ He

☐ It

☐ She

3.5) Which word can replace 'the girls'?

☐ It

☐ He

☐ They

☐ She

3.6) Which word can replace 'my mom'?

☐ It

☐ They

☐ She

☐ He

3.7) Which word can replace 'the dog'?

☐ It

☐ She

☐ They

☐ He

3.8) Which word can replace 'my dad'?

☐ She

☐ They

☐ He

☐ It

3.9) Which word can replace 'the children'?

☐ He

☐ She

☐ They

☐ It

3.10) Which word can replace 'my sister'?

☐ They

☐ It

☐ He

☐ She

3.11) Which word can replace 'Sarah and John'?

☐ She

☐ It

☐ They

☐ He

3.12) Choose the correct pronoun for 'the bird'.

☐ It

☐ He

☐ She

☐ They

3.13) Which pronoun replaces 'my friends'?

☐ She

☐ It

☐ He

☐ They

3.14) Which word can replace 'the books'?

☐ It

☐ He

☐ They

☐ She

3.15) Choose the correct pronoun for 'the teacher'.

☐ They

☐ He

☐ She

☐ It

3.16) Which word can replace 'the apple'?

☐ She

☐ He

☐ They

☐ It

3.17) Which pronoun replaces 'the car'?

☐ He

☐ It

☐ She

☐ They

3.18) Choose the correct pronoun for 'my brothers'.

☐ She

☐ He

☐ They

☐ It

3.19) Which word can replace 'the trees'?

☐ She

☐ It

☐ They

☐ He

3.20) Choose the correct pronoun for 'the girl'.

☐ She

☐ It

☐ They

☐ He

3.21) Which word can replace 'the kids'?

☐ She

☐ They

☐ He

☐ It

3.22) Choose the correct pronoun for 'the woman'.

☐ It

☐ She

☐ He

☐ They

3.23) Which pronoun replaces 'the animals'?

☐ He

☐ It

☐ They

☐ She

3.24) Which word can replace 'the ball'?

☐ She

☐ They

☐ He

☐ It

3.25) Choose the correct pronoun for 'my friends and I'.

☐ We

☐ They

☐ He

☐ She

3.26) Which word can replace 'the stars'?

☐ She

☐ He

☐ It

☐ They

3.27) Which pronoun replaces 'the baby'?

☐ He

☐ They

☐ It

☐ She

3.28) Choose the correct pronoun for 'my brother and I'.

☐ She

☐ We

☐ He

☐ They

3.29) Which word can replace 'the books and the pens'?

☐ He

☐ They

☐ She

☐ It

3.30) Choose the correct pronoun for 'the man'.

☐ She

☐ He

☐ It

☐ They

3.31) Which word can replace 'the dogs'?

☐ They

☐ It

☐ He

☐ She

3.32) Choose the correct pronoun for 'the boy'.

☐ He

☐ They

☐ She

☐ It

3.33) Which pronoun replaces 'my parents'?

☐ They

☐ He

☐ She

☐ It

3.34) Which word can replace 'the book'?

☐ It

☐ They

☐ He

☐ She

3.35) Choose the correct pronoun for 'my sister and I'.

☐ She

☐ They

☐ We

☐ He

3.36) Which word can replace 'the flowers'?

☐ She

☐ It

☐ They

☐ He

3.37) Which pronoun replaces 'the pencil'?

☐ It

☐ She

☐ He

☐ They

3.38) Choose the correct pronoun for 'the children'.

☐ They

☐ It

☐ He

☐ She

3.39) Which word can replace 'the moon'?

☐ It

☐ They

☐ He

☐ She

3.40) Choose the correct pronoun for 'my teacher'.

☐ She

☐ It

☐ He

☐ They

Topic 3 - Answers

Question Number	Answer	Explanation
3.1	He	'Tom' is a male proper noun and is replaced by the pronoun 'He'.
3.2	She	'Lisa' is a female proper noun and is replaced by the pronoun 'She'.
3.3	It	'The cat' is a non-human noun and is replaced by the pronoun 'It'.
3.4	They	'The boys' is a plural noun and is replaced by the pronoun 'They'.
3.5	They	'The girls' is a plural noun and is replaced by the pronoun 'They'.
3.6	She	'My mom' is a female noun and is replaced by the pronoun 'She'.
3.7	It	'The dog' is a non-human noun and is replaced by the pronoun 'It'.
3.8	He	'My dad' is a male noun and is replaced by the pronoun 'He'.
3.9	They	'The children' is a plural noun and is replaced by the pronoun 'They'.
3.10	She	'My sister' is a female noun and is replaced by the pronoun 'She'.
3.11	They	'Sarah and John' is a plural noun and is replaced by the pronoun 'They'.
3.12	It	'The bird' is a non-human noun and is replaced by the pronoun 'It'.
3.13	They	'My friends' is a plural noun and is replaced by the pronoun 'They'.
3.14	They	'The books' is a plural noun and is replaced by the pronoun 'They'.
3.15	He/She	'The teacher' can be either male or female and is replaced by 'He' or 'She'.
3.16	It	'The apple' is a non-human noun and is replaced by the pronoun 'It'.
3.17	It	'The car' is a non-human noun and is replaced by the pronoun 'It'.
3.18	They	'My brothers' is a plural noun and is replaced by the pronoun 'They'.

3.19	They	'The trees' is a plural noun and is replaced by the pronoun 'They'.
3.20	She	'The girl' is a female noun and is replaced by the pronoun 'She'.
3.21	They	'The kids' is a plural noun and is replaced by the pronoun 'They'.
3.22	She	'The woman' is a female noun and is replaced by the pronoun 'She'.
3.23	They	'The animals' is a plural noun and is replaced by the pronoun 'They'.
3.24	It	'The ball' is a non-human noun and is replaced by the pronoun 'It'.
3.25	We	'My friends and I' is a plural noun and is replaced by the pronoun 'We'.
3.26	They	'The stars' is a plural noun and is replaced by the pronoun 'They'.
3.27	It	'The baby' is a non-specific gender noun and is replaced by 'It'.
3.28	We	'My brother and I' is a plural noun and is replaced by 'We'.
3.29	They	'The books and the pens' is a plural noun and is replaced by 'They'.
3.30	He	'The man' is a male noun and is replaced by the pronoun 'He'.
3.31	They	'The dogs' is a plural noun and is replaced by the pronoun 'They'.
3.32	He	'The boy' is a male noun and is replaced by the pronoun 'He'.
3.33	They	'My parents' is a plural noun and is replaced by the pronoun 'They'.
3.34	It	'The book' is a non-human noun and is replaced by the pronoun 'It'.
3.35	We	'My sister and I' is a plural noun and is replaced by 'We'.
3.36	They	'The flowers' is a plural noun and is replaced by the pronoun 'They'.
3.37	It	'The pencil' is a non-human noun and is replaced by the pronoun 'It'.
3.38	They	'The children' is a plural noun and is replaced by the pronoun 'They'.
3.39	It	'The moon' is a non-human noun and is replaced by the pronoun 'It'.
3.40	He/She	'My teacher' can be either male or female and is replaced by 'He' or 'She'.

Topic 4 - Adjectives

4.1) Which word describes something big?

☐ Round

☐ Huge

☐ Fast

☐ Tiny

4.2) Which word describes something happy?

☐ Sad

☐ Quiet

☐ Angry

☐ Joyful

4.3) Which word describes something small?

☐ Heavy

☐ Large

☐ Bright

☐ Little

4.4) Which word describes something fast?

☐ Hard

☐ Quick

☐ Slow

☐ Soft

4.5) Which word describes something cold?

☐ Furry

☐ Chilly

☐ Hot

☐ Warm

4.6) Which word describes something loud?

☐ Silent

☐ Noisy

☐ Calm

☐ Smooth

4.7) Which word describes something soft?

☐ Bumpy

☐ Rough

☐ Gentle

☐ Sharp

4.8) Which word describes something tall?

☐ Short

☐ Narrow

☐ Wide

☐ High

4.9) Which word describes something sweet?

- ☐ Sugary
- ☐ Sour
- ☐ Salty
- ☐ Bitter

4.10) Which word describes something bright?

- ☐ Dull
- ☐ Dark
- ☐ Damp
- ☐ Shiny

4.11) Which word describes something wet?

- ☐ Soft
- ☐ Dry
- ☐ Damp
- ☐ Light

4.12) Which word describes something dark?

- ☐ Loud
- ☐ Bright
- ☐ Quiet
- ☐ Gloomy

4.13) Which word describes something round?

- ☐ Flat
- ☐ Circular
- ☐ Pointy
- ☐ Square

4.14) Which word describes something quiet?

- ☐ Loud
- ☐ Silent
- ☐ Noisy
- ☐ Bumpy

4.15) Which word describes something smooth?

- ☐ Silky
- ☐ Rough
- ☐ Sharp
- ☐ Hard

4.16) Which word describes something heavy?

- ☐ Thin
- ☐ Light
- ☐ Tiny
- ☐ Weighty

4.17) Which word describes something thin?

☐ Slim

☐ Wide

☐ Thick

☐ Deep

4.18) Which word describes something soft?

☐ Cushy

☐ Tough

☐ Hard

☐ Rough

4.19) Which word describes something clean?

☐ Spotless

☐ Messy

☐ Dirty

☐ Muddy

4.20) Which word describes something shiny?

☐ Glittery

☐ Dull

☐ Dim

☐ Matte

4.21) Which word describes something broken?

☐ Fixed

☐ New

☐ Perfect

☐ Damaged

4.22) Which word describes something warm?

☐ Hot

☐ Frozen

☐ Icy

☐ Cool

4.23) Which word describes something colorful?

☐ Dark

☐ Dull

☐ Plain

☐ Vibrant

4.24) Which word describes something quiet?

☐ Silent

☐ Loud

☐ Echoing

☐ Noisy

4.25) Which word describes something tall?

☐ Wide

☐ Short

☐ High

☐ Narrow

4.26) Which word describes something fluffy?

☐ Soft

☐ Smooth

☐ Hard

☐ Rough

4.27) Which word describes something light?

☐ Dim

☐ Bright

☐ Heavy

☐ Dark

4.28) Which word describes something new?

☐ Fresh

☐ Ancient

☐ Used

☐ Old

4.29) Which word describes something dry?

☐ Wet

☐ Soaked

☐ Moist

☐ Arid

4.30) Which word describes something cold?

☐ Chilly

☐ Hot

☐ Toasty

☐ Warm

4.31) Which word describes something sticky?

☐ Fluffy

☐ Adhesive

☐ Dry

☐ Smooth

4.32) Which word describes something sleepy?

☐ Energetic

☐ Awake

☐ Alert

☐ Tired

4.33) Which word describes something brave?

☐ Scared

☐ Afraid

☐ Timid

☐ Courageous

4.34) Which word describes something hungry?

☐ Satisfied

☐ Stuffed

☐ Starving

☐ Full

4.35) Which word describes something shiny?

☐ Dull

☐ Glittering

☐ Dark

☐ Dim

4.36) Which word describes something kind?

☐ Mean

☐ Angry

☐ Rude

☐ Friendly

4.37) Which word describes something funny?

- ☐ Humorous
- ☐ Sad
- ☐ Boring
- ☐ Serious

4.38) Which word describes something lazy?

- ☐ Active
- ☐ Busy
- ☐ Idle
- ☐ Energetic

4.39) Which word describes something careful?

- ☐ Hasty
- ☐ Reckless
- ☐ Careless
- ☐ Cautious

4.40) Which word describes something messy?

- ☐ Organized
- ☐ Untidy
- ☐ Neat
- ☐ Clean

Topic 4 - Answers

Question Number	Answer	Explanation
4.1	Huge	'Huge' describes something big.
4.2	Joyful	'Joyful' describes something happy.
4.3	Little	'Little' describes something small.
4.4	Quick	'Quick' describes something fast.
4.5	Chilly	'Chilly' describes something cold.
4.6	Noisy	'Noisy' describes something loud.
4.7	Gentle	'Gentle' describes something soft.
4.8	High	'High' describes something tall.
4.9	Sugary	'Sugary' describes something sweet.
4.10	Shiny	'Shiny' describes something bright.
4.11	Damp	'Damp' describes something wet.
4.12	Gloomy	'Gloomy' describes something dark.
4.13	Circular	'Circular' describes something round.
4.14	Silent	'Silent' describes something quiet.
4.15	Silky	'Silky' describes something smooth.
4.16	Weighty	'Weighty' describes something heavy.
4.17	Slim	'Slim' describes something thin.
4.18	Cushy	'Cushy' describes something soft.

4.19	Spotless	'Spotless' describes something clean.
4.20	Glittery	'Glittery' describes something shiny.
4.21	Damaged	'Damaged' describes something broken.
4.22	Cool	'Cool' describes something warm.
4.23	Vibrant	'Vibrant' describes something colorful.
4.24	Silent	'Silent' describes something quiet.
4.25	High	'High' describes something tall.
4.26	Soft	'Soft' describes something fluffy.
4.27	Bright	'Bright' describes something light.
4.28	Fresh	'Fresh' describes something new.
4.29	Arid	'Arid' describes something dry.
4.30	Chilly	'Chilly' describes something cold.
4.31	Adhesive	'Adhesive' describes something sticky.
4.32	Tired	'Tired' describes something sleepy.
4.33	Courageous	'Courageous' describes something brave.
4.34	Starving	'Starving' describes something hungry.
4.35	Glittering	'Glittering' describes something shiny.
4.36	Friendly	'Friendly' describes something kind.
4.37	Humorous	'Humorous' describes something funny.
4.38	Idle	'Idle' describes something lazy.
4.39	Cautious	'Cautious' describes something careful.
4.40	Untidy	'Untidy' describes something messy.

Topic 5 - Word Meaning

5.1) What is the meaning of 'happy'?

☐ Joyful

☐ Sad

☐ Quiet

☐ Angry

5.2) What is the meaning of 'big'?

☐ Small

☐ Large

☐ Little

☐ Tiny

5.3) What is the meaning of 'run'?

☐ Walk slowly

☐ Move fast

☐ Jump high

☐ Sit down

5.4) What is the meaning of 'cold'?

☐ Chilly

☐ Warm

☐ Furry

☐ Hot

5.5) What is the meaning of 'bright'?

☐ Dull

☐ Dark

☐ Dim

☐ Shiny

5.6) What is the meaning of 'soft'?

☐ Bumpy

☐ Hard

☐ Gentle

☐ Rough

5.7) What is the meaning of 'clean'?

☐ Muddy

☐ Dirty

☐ Messy

☐ Spotless

5.8) What is the meaning of 'quick'?

☐ Slow

☐ Heavy

☐ Fast

☐ Light

5.9) What is the meaning of 'laugh'?

☐ Giggle

☐ Yell

☐ Cry

☐ Whisper

5.10) What is the meaning of 'tall'?

☐ High

☐ Wide

☐ Narrow

☐ Short

5.11) What is the meaning of 'small'?

☐ Tiny

☐ Huge

☐ Fast

☐ Round

5.12) What is the meaning of 'angry'?

☐ Mad

☐ Calm

☐ Happy

☐ Excited

5.13) What is the meaning of 'jump'?

☐ Walk

☐ Leap

☐ Sit

☐ Stand

5.14) What is the meaning of 'warm'?

☐ Cold

☐ Cool

☐ Freezing

☐ Hot

5.15) What is the meaning of 'loud'?

☐ Soft

☐ Noisy

☐ Quiet

☐ Silent

5.16) What is the meaning of 'rough'?

☐ Bumpy

☐ Smooth

☐ Gentle

☐ Soft

5.17) What is the meaning of 'heavy'?

☐ Tiny

☐ Light

☐ Weighty

☐ Thin

5.18) What is the meaning of 'thin'?

☐ Wide

☐ Thick

☐ Deep

☐ Slim

5.19) What is the meaning of 'fast'?

☐ Slow

☐ Quick

☐ Lazy

☐ Tired

5.20) What is the meaning of 'wet'?

☐ Soft

☐ Light

☐ Dry

☐ Damp

5.21) What is the meaning of 'hungry'?

☐ Starving

☐ Satisfied

☐ Full

☐ Stuffed

5.22) What is the meaning of 'brave'?

☐ Scared

☐ Afraid

☐ Courageous

☐ Timid

5.23) What is the meaning of 'sad'?

☐ Excited

☐ Unhappy

☐ Calm

☐ Joyful

5.24) What is the meaning of 'dry'?

☐ Sticky

☐ Not wet

☐ Wet

☐ Soft

5.25) What is the meaning of 'quiet'?

☐ Echoing

☐ Loud

☐ Noisy

☐ Silent

5.26) What is the meaning of 'sleepy'?

☐ Energetic

☐ Alert

☐ Tired

☐ Awake

5.27) What is the meaning of 'slow'?

☐ Quick

☐ Speedy

☐ Not fast

☐ Swift

5.28) What is the meaning of 'kind'?

☐ Mean

☐ Angry

☐ Rude

☐ Friendly

5.29) What is the meaning of 'funny'?

☐ Serious

☐ Sad

☐ Boring

☐ Humorous

5.30) What is the meaning of 'tired'?

☐ Energetic

☐ Sleepy

☐ Awake

☐ Active

5.31) What is the meaning of 'new'?

☐ Fresh

☐ Used

☐ Old

☐ Ancient

5.32) What is the meaning of 'lazy'?

☐ Active

☐ Energetic

☐ Busy

☐ Idle

5.33) What is the meaning of 'careful'?

☐ Cautious

☐ Hasty

☐ Careless

☐ Reckless

5.34) What is the meaning of 'dark'?

☐ Bright

☐ Loud

☐ Gloomy

☐ Quiet

5.35) What is the meaning of 'giggle'?

☐ Shout

☐ Whisper

☐ Cry loudly

☐ Laugh lightly

5.36) What is the meaning of 'crawl'?

☐ Walk slowly

☐ Move on hands and knees

☐ Jump high

☐ Run fast

5.37) What is the meaning of 'float'?

☐ Dive

☐ Sink

☐ Stay on the surface of water

☐ Swim quickly

5.38) What is the meaning of 'shine'?

☐ Be dark

☐ Give off light

☐ Be dull

☐ Hide

5.39) What is the meaning of 'whisper'?

☐ Shout

☐ Laugh

☐ Cry

☐ Speak softly

5.40) What is the meaning of 'gather'?

☐ Hide

☐ Collect together

☐ Scatter

☐ Separate

Topic 5 - Answers

Question Number	Answer	Explanation
5.1	Joyful	'Joyful' is a synonym for 'happy'.
5.2	Large	'Large' is a synonym for 'big'.
5.3	Move fast	'Run' means to move fast.
5.4	Chilly	'Chilly' is a synonym for 'cold'.
5.5	Shiny	'Shiny' is a synonym for 'bright'.
5.6	Gentle	'Gentle' is a synonym for 'soft'.
5.7	Spotless	'Spotless' is a synonym for 'clean'.
5.8	Fast	'Fast' is a synonym for 'quick'.
5.9	Giggle	'Giggle' is a synonym for 'laugh'.
5.10	High	'High' is a synonym for 'tall'.
5.11	Tiny	'Tiny' is a synonym for 'small'.
5.12	Mad	'Mad' is a synonym for 'angry'.
5.13	Leap	'Leap' is a synonym for 'jump'.
5.14	Hot	'Hot' is a synonym for 'warm'.
5.15	Noisy	'Noisy' is a synonym for 'loud'.
5.16	Bumpy	'Bumpy' is a synonym for 'rough'.
5.17	Weighty	'Weighty' is a synonym for 'heavy'.
5.18	Slim	'Slim' is a synonym for 'thin'.

5.19	Quick	'Quick' is a synonym for 'fast'.
5.20	Damp	'Damp' is a synonym for 'wet'.
5.21	Starving	'Starving' is a synonym for 'hungry'.
5.22	Courageous	'Courageous' is a synonym for 'brave'.
5.23	Unhappy	'Unhappy' is a synonym for 'sad'.
5.24	Not wet	'Not wet' is a definition for 'dry'.
5.25	Silent	'Silent' is a synonym for 'quiet'.
5.26	Tired	'Tired' is a synonym for 'sleepy'.
5.27	Not fast	'Not fast' is a definition for 'slow'.
5.28	Friendly	'Friendly' is a synonym for 'kind'.
5.29	Humorous	'Humorous' is a synonym for 'funny'.
5.30	Sleepy	'Sleepy' is a synonym for 'tired'.
5.31	Fresh	'Fresh' is a synonym for 'new'.
5.32	Idle	'Idle' is a synonym for 'lazy'.
5.33	Cautious	'Cautious' is a synonym for 'careful'.
5.34	Gloomy	'Gloomy' is a synonym for 'dark'.
5.35	Laugh lightly	'Laugh lightly' is a synonym for 'giggle'.
5.36	Move on hands and knees	'Move on hands and knees' is a definition for 'crawl'.
5.37	Stay on the surface of water	'Stay on the surface of water' is a definition for 'float'.
5.38	Give off light	'Give off light' is a definition for 'shine'.
5.39	Speak softly	'Speak softly' is a synonym for 'whisper'.
5.40	Collect together	'Collect together' is a definition for 'gather'.

Topic 6 – Nouns

6.1) Which one is a noun?

☐ Cat

☐ Happy

☐ Run

☐ Quick

6.2) Which word is a person?

☐ Jump

☐ Blue

☐ Teacher

☐ Fast

6.3) Which one is a place?

☐ Quickly

☐ Loud

☐ School

☐ Running

6.4) Which one is a thing?

☐ Bright

☐ Book

☐ Sing

☐ Easily

6.5) Which word is an animal?

☐ Dog

☐ Green

☐ Sleep

☐ Quickly

6.6) Which one is a noun?

☐ Tree

☐ Run

☐ Angry

☐ Slowly

6.7) Which word is a person?

☐ Doctor

☐ Quick

☐ Happy

☐ Jump

6.8) Which one is a place?

☐ Singing

☐ Bright

☐ Park

☐ Fast

6.9) Which one is a thing?

☐ Slow

☐ Sad

☐ Laugh

☐ Chair

6.10) Which word is an animal?

☐ Quietly

☐ Bird

☐ Talk

☐ Red

6.11) Which one is a person?

☐ Blue

☐ Run

☐ Bright

☐ Nurse

6.12) Which word is a thing?

☐ Happy

☐ Swim

☐ Pencil

☐ Slow

6.13) Which one is a place?

- ☐ Library
- ☐ Running
- ☐ Green
- ☐ Jump

6.14) Which one is an animal?

- ☐ Loudly
- ☐ Red
- ☐ Talk
- ☐ Elephant

6.15) Which one is a noun?

- ☐ Quick
- ☐ Sing
- ☐ Car
- ☐ Joyful

6.16) Which word is a person?

- ☐ Yellow
- ☐ Sleep
- ☐ Quickly
- ☐ Firefighter

6.17) Which one is a thing?

☐ Sad

☐ Laugh

☐ Quick

☐ Desk

6.18) Which word is an animal?

☐ Talk

☐ Lion

☐ Fast

☐ Quietly

6.19) Which one is a place?

☐ Running

☐ Jump

☐ Zoo

☐ Bright

6.20) Which one is a noun?

☐ Bicycle

☐ Slowly

☐ Sing

☐ Angry

6.21) Which one is a person?

☐ Farmer

☐ Cry

☐ Fast

☐ Green

6.22) Which word is a thing?

☐ Jump

☐ Table

☐ Happy

☐ Sing

6.23) Which one is a place?

☐ Running

☐ Bright

☐ Blue

☐ Beach

6.24) Which one is an animal?

☐ Talk

☐ Cat

☐ Loudly

☐ Red

6.25) Which one is a noun?

☐ Dance

☐ House

☐ Quick

☐ Sad

6.26) Which word is a person?

☐ Quickly

☐ Sleep

☐ Yellow

☐ Pilot

6.27) Which one is a thing?

☐ Quick

☐ Sad

☐ Laugh

☐ Window

6.28) Which word is an animal?

☐ Fish

☐ Quietly

☐ Fast

☐ Talk

6.29) Which one is a place?

☐ Jump

☐ Bright

☐ Running

☐ Hospital

6.30) Which one is a noun?

☐ Angry

☐ Toy

☐ Sing

☐ Slowly

6.31) Which one is a person?

☐ Fast

☐ Bright

☐ Cry

☐ Chef

6.32) Which word is a thing?

☐ Sing

☐ Happy

☐ Jump

☐ Cup

6.33) Which one is a place?

☐ Mall

☐ Bright

☐ Blue

☐ Running

6.34) Which one is an animal?

☐ Red

☐ Rabbit

☐ Loudly

☐ Talk

6.35) Which one is a noun?

☐ Dance

☐ Sad

☐ Quick

☐ Carpet

6.36) Which word is a person?

☐ Sleep

☐ Driver

☐ Quickly

☐ Yellow

6.37) Which one is a thing?

☐ Quick

☐ Laugh

☐ Laptop

☐ Sad

6.38) Which word is an animal?

☐ Turtle

☐ Quietly

☐ Fast

☐ Talk

6.39) Which one is a place?

☐ Jump

☐ Running

☐ Bright

☐ Airport

6.40) Which one is a noun?

☐ Slowly

☐ Shoes

☐ Angry

☐ Sing

Topic 6 - Answers

Question Number	Answer	Explanation
6.1	Cat	'Cat' is a noun.
6.2	Teacher	'Teacher' is a noun referring to a person.
6.3	School	'School' is a noun referring to a place.
6.4	Book	'Book' is a noun referring to a thing.
6.5	Dog	'Dog' is a noun referring to an animal.
6.6	Tree	'Tree' is a noun.
6.7	Doctor	'Doctor' is a noun referring to a person.
6.8	Park	'Park' is a noun referring to a place.
6.9	Chair	'Chair' is a noun referring to a thing.
6.10	Bird	'Bird' is a noun referring to an animal.
6.11	Nurse	'Nurse' is a noun referring to a person.
6.12	Pencil	'Pencil' is a noun referring to a thing.
6.13	Library	'Library' is a noun referring to a place.
6.14	Elephant	'Elephant' is a noun referring to an animal.
6.15	Car	'Car' is a noun.
6.16	Firefighter	'Firefighter' is a noun referring to a person.
6.17	Desk	'Desk' is a noun referring to a thing.
6.18	Lion	'Lion' is a noun referring to an animal.

6.19	Zoo	'Zoo' is a noun referring to a place.
6.20	Bicycle	'Bicycle' is a noun.
6.21	Farmer	'Farmer' is a noun referring to a person.
6.22	Table	'Table' is a noun referring to a thing.
6.23	Beach	'Beach' is a noun referring to a place.
6.24	Cat	'Cat' is a noun referring to an animal.
6.25	House	'House' is a noun.
6.26	Pilot	'Pilot' is a noun referring to a person.
6.27	Window	'Window' is a noun referring to a thing.
6.28	Fish	'Fish' is a noun referring to an animal.
6.29	Hospital	'Hospital' is a noun referring to a place.
6.30	Toy	'Toy' is a noun.
6.31	Chef	'Chef' is a noun referring to a person.
6.32	Cup	'Cup' is a noun referring to a thing.
6.33	Mall	'Mall' is a noun referring to a place.
6.34	Rabbit	'Rabbit' is a noun referring to an animal.
6.35	Carpet	'Carpet' is a noun.
6.36	Driver	'Driver' is a noun referring to a person.
6.37	Laptop	'Laptop' is a noun referring to a thing.
6.38	Turtle	'Turtle' is a noun referring to an animal.
6.39	Airport	'Airport' is a noun referring to a place.
6.40	Shoes	'Shoes' is a noun.

Topic 7 - Tenses

7.1) What is the past tense of 'run'?

☐ Runs

☐ Run

☐ Ran

☐ Running

7.2) What is the present tense of 'played'?

☐ Played

☐ Plays

☐ Playing

☐ Play

7.3) What is the future tense of 'eat'?

☐ Eats

☐ Eating

☐ Will eat

☐ Ate

7.4) What is the past tense of 'jump'?

☐ Jumps

☐ Jumping

☐ Jumped

☐ Jump

7.5) What is the present tense of 'slept'?

☐ Sleeping

☐ Sleep

☐ Sleeps

☐ Slept

7.6) What is the future tense of 'sing'?

☐ Sang

☐ Singing

☐ Will sing

☐ Sings

7.7) What is the past tense of 'dance'?

☐ Danced

☐ Dancing

☐ Dances

☐ Dance

7.8) What is the present tense of 'went'?

☐ Goes

☐ Go

☐ Going

☐ Went

7.9) What is the future tense of 'read'?

☐ Will read

☐ Read

☐ Reads

☐ Reading

7.10) What is the past tense of 'swim'?

☐ Swimming

☐ Swims

☐ Swam

☐ Swim

7.11) What is the past tense of 'walk'?

☐ Walk

☐ Walking

☐ Walked

☐ Walks

7.12) What is the present tense of 'played'?

☐ Playing

☐ Play

☐ Plays

☐ Played

7.13) What is the future tense of 'write'?

☐ Wrote

☐ Writing

☐ Will write

☐ Writes

7.14) What is the past tense of 'talk'?

☐ Talk

☐ Talking

☐ Talked

☐ Talks

7.15) What is the present tense of 'sang'?

☐ Sings

☐ Sang

☐ Singing

☐ Sing

7.16) What is the future tense of 'run'?

☐ Will run

☐ Running

☐ Ran

☐ Runs

7.17) What is the past tense of 'climb'?

☐ Climbs

☐ Climb

☐ Climbing

☐ Climbed

7.18) What is the present tense of 'jumped'?

☐ Jumping

☐ Jump

☐ Jumps

☐ Jumped

7.19) What is the future tense of 'draw'?

☐ Drew

☐ Drawing

☐ Will draw

☐ Draws

7.20) What is the past tense of 'fly'?

☐ Flying

☐ Fly

☐ Flies

☐ Flew

7.21) What is the past tense of 'read'?

☐ Reads

☐ Reading

☐ Read

☐ Reader

7.22) What is the present tense of 'ate'?

☐ Eaten

☐ Eats

☐ Eat

☐ Eating

7.23) What is the future tense of 'sleep'?

☐ Sleeping

☐ Slept

☐ Will sleep

☐ Sleeps

7.24) What is the past tense of 'draw'?

☐ Drawing

☐ Drawn

☐ Draws

☐ Drew

7.25) What is the present tense of 'ran'?

☐ Running

☐ Run

☐ Runs

☐ Ran

7.26) What is the future tense of 'talk'?

☐ Talking

☐ Talks

☐ Talked

☐ Will talk

7.27) What is the past tense of 'write'?

☐ Written

☐ Writes

☐ Writing

☐ Wrote

7.28) What is the present tense of 'played'?

☐ Playing

☐ Play

☐ Plays

☐ Played

7.29) What is the future tense of 'jump'?

☐ Will jump

☐ Jumps

☐ Jumped

☐ Jumping

7.30) What is the past tense of 'sing'?

☐ Singing

☐ Sings

☐ Sang

☐ Sing

7.31) What is the past tense of 'buy'?

☐ Buys

☐ Buying

☐ Bought

☐ Buy

7.32) What is the present tense of 'slept'?

☐ Sleeping

☐ Sleep

☐ Sleeps

☐ Slept

7.33) What is the future tense of 'drink'?

☐ Drinking

☐ Drinks

☐ Will drink

☐ Drank

7.34) What is the past tense of 'see'?

☐ Saw

☐ Seen

☐ Seeing

☐ Sees

7.35) What is the present tense of 'went'?

☐ Go

☐ Goes

☐ Went

☐ Going

7.36) What is the future tense of 'run'?

☐ Will run

☐ Ran

☐ Runs

☐ Running

7.37) What is the past tense of 'give'?

☐ Giving

☐ Gave

☐ Gives

☐ Give

7.38) What is the present tense of 'fell'?

☐ Falls

☐ Falling

☐ Fall

☐ Fell

7.39) What is the future tense of 'find'?

☐ Finds

☐ Finding

☐ Found

☐ Will find

7.40) What is the past tense of 'eat'?

☐ Eating

☐ Eats

☐ Ate

☐ Eaten

Topic 7 - Answers

Question Number	Answer	Explanation
7.1	Ran	'Ran' is the past tense of 'run'.
7.2	Play	'Play' is the present tense of 'played'.
7.3	Will eat	'Will eat' is the future tense of 'eat'.
7.4	Jumped	'Jumped' is the past tense of 'jump'.
7.5	Sleep	'Sleep' is the present tense of 'slept'.
7.6	Will sing	'Will sing' is the future tense of 'sing'.
7.7	Danced	'Danced' is the past tense of 'dance'.
7.8	Goes	'Goes' is the present tense of 'went'.
7.9	Will read	'Will read' is the future tense of 'read'.
7.10	Swam	'Swam' is the past tense of 'swim'.
7.11	Walked	'Walked' is the past tense of 'walk'.
7.12	Play	'Play' is the present tense of 'played'.
7.13	Will write	'Will write' is the future tense of 'write'.
7.14	Talked	'Talked' is the past tense of 'talk'.
7.15	Sings	'Sings' is the present tense of 'sang'.
7.16	Will run	'Will run' is the future tense of 'run'.
7.17	Climbed	'Climbed' is the past tense of 'climb'.
7.18	Jumps	'Jumps' is the present tense of 'jumped'.

7.19	Will draw	'Will draw' is the future tense of 'draw'.
7.20	Flew	'Flew' is the past tense of 'fly'.
7.21	Read	'Read' is the past tense of 'read'.
7.22	Eats	'Eats' is the present tense of 'ate'.
7.23	Will sleep	'Will sleep' is the future tense of 'sleep'.
7.24	Drew	'Drew' is the past tense of 'draw'.
7.25	Runs	'Runs' is the present tense of 'ran'.
7.26	Will talk	'Will talk' is the future tense of 'talk'.
7.27	Wrote	'Wrote' is the past tense of 'write'.
7.28	Play	'Play' is the present tense of 'played'.
7.29	Will jump	'Will jump' is the future tense of 'jump'.
7.30	Sang	'Sang' is the past tense of 'sing'.
7.31	Bought	'Bought' is the past tense of 'buy'.
7.32	Sleeps	'Sleeps' is the present tense of 'slept'.
7.33	Will drink	'Will drink' is the future tense of 'drink'.
7.34	Saw	'Saw' is the past tense of 'see'.
7.35	Goes	'Goes' is the present tense of 'went'.
7.36	Will run	'Will run' is the future tense of 'run'.
7.37	Gave	'Gave' is the past tense of 'give'.
7.38	Falls	'Falls' is the present tense of 'fell'.
7.39	Will find	'Will find' is the future tense of 'find'.
7.40	Ate	'Ate' is the past tense of 'eat'.

Topic 8 - Prepositions

8.1) What is the preposition in this sentence: 'The cat is on the mat.'?

☐ On

☐ Cat

☐ Mat

☐ Is

8.2) Which word is a preposition?

☐ Happy

☐ Under

☐ Quick

☐ Run

8.3) What is the preposition: 'The book is under the table.'?

☐ Under

☐ Book

☐ Is

☐ Table

8.4) Which word is a preposition?

☐ Behind

☐ Red

☐ Jump

☐ Soft

8.5) What is the preposition in this sentence: 'The dog is in the house.'?

☐ In

☐ Dog

☐ Is

☐ House

8.6) Which word is a preposition?

☐ Laugh

☐ Above

☐ Fast

☐ Green

8.7) What is the preposition in this sentence: 'The ball is next to the chair.'?

☐ Ball

☐ Next to

☐ Chair

☐ Is

8.8) Which word is a preposition?

☐ Blue

☐ Happy

☐ Dance

☐ Between

8.9) What is the preposition in this sentence: 'The car is beside the tree.'?

☐ Tree

☐ Is

☐ Car

☐ Beside

8.10) Which word is a preposition?

☐ Yellow

☐ Over

☐ Jump

☐ Sing

8.11) What is the preposition in this sentence: 'The bird is in the cage.'?

☐ Cage

☐ Is

☐ Bird

☐ In

8.12) Which word is a preposition?

☐ Happy

☐ Soft

☐ Near

☐ Run

8.13) What is the preposition in this sentence: 'The cat is between the chairs.'?

☐ Chairs

☐ Cat

☐ Between

☐ Is

8.14) Which word is a preposition?

☐ Quick

☐ Jump

☐ Blue

☐ Through

8.15) What is the preposition in this sentence: 'The book is on the table.'?

☐ Book

☐ On

☐ Is

☐ Table

8.16) Which word is a preposition?

☐ Under

☐ Sing

☐ Green

☐ Fast

8.17) What is the preposition in this sentence: 'The ball is beside the desk.'?

☐ Ball

☐ Beside

☐ Is

☐ Desk

8.18) Which word is a preposition?

☐ Yellow

☐ Behind

☐ Dance

☐ Happy

8.19) What is the preposition in this sentence: 'The car is near the house.'?

☐ Is

☐ Car

☐ Near

☐ House

8.20) Which word is a preposition?

☐ Run

☐ Red

☐ Jump

☐ Above

8.21) What is the preposition in this sentence: 'The fish is under the water.'?

☐ Water

☐ Under

☐ Fish

☐ Is

8.22) Which word is a preposition?

☐ Soft

☐ With

☐ Happy

☐ Run

8.23) What is the preposition in this sentence: 'The ball is behind the door.'?

☐ Behind

☐ Ball

☐ Door

☐ Is

8.24) Which word is a preposition?

☐ Jump

☐ Quick

☐ Inside

☐ Blue

8.25) What is the preposition in this sentence: 'The bird flew above the tree.'?

- ☐ Bird
- ☐ Flew
- ☐ Tree
- ☐ Above

8.26) Which word is a preposition?

- ☐ Sing
- ☐ Fast
- ☐ Green
- ☐ Across

8.27) What is the preposition in this sentence: 'The cat is beside the dog.'?

- ☐ Dog
- ☐ Beside
- ☐ Is
- ☐ Cat

8.28) Which word is a preposition?

- ☐ Around
- ☐ Yellow
- ☐ Happy
- ☐ Dance

8.29) What is the preposition in this sentence: 'The book is next to the lamp.'?

☐ Next to

☐ Book

☐ Lamp

☐ Is

8.30) Which word is a preposition?

☐ Red

☐ Run

☐ Jump

☐ Among

8.31) What is the preposition in this sentence: 'The dog is next to the cat.'?

☐ Next to

☐ Is

☐ Dog

☐ Cat

8.32) Which word is a preposition?

☐ Happy

☐ Near

☐ Soft

☐ Run

8.33) What is the preposition in this sentence: 'The pen is on the table.'?

- Is
- On
- Pen
- Table

8.34) Which word is a preposition?

- Blue
- Quick
- Beside
- Jump

8.35) What is the preposition in this sentence: 'The girl walked across the street.'?

- Street
- Walked
- Girl
- Across

8.36) Which word is a preposition?

- Sing
- Between
- Fast
- Green

8.37) What is the preposition in this sentence: 'The apple is in the basket.'?

☐ Apple

☐ In

☐ Is

☐ Basket

8.38) Which word is a preposition?

☐ Yellow

☐ Dance

☐ Happy

☐ Underneath

8.39) What is the preposition in this sentence: 'The bird flew over the house.'?

☐ House

☐ Flew

☐ Bird

☐ Over

8.40) Which word is a preposition?

☐ Red

☐ Among

☐ Run

☐ Jump

Topic 8 - Answers

Question Number	Answer	Explanation
8.1	On	'On' is a preposition.
8.2	Under	'Under' is a preposition.
8.3	Under	'Under' is a preposition.
8.4	Behind	'Behind' is a preposition.
8.5	In	'In' is a preposition.
8.6	Above	'Above' is a preposition.
8.7	Next to	'Next to' is a preposition.
8.8	Between	'Between' is a preposition.
8.9	Beside	'Beside' is a preposition.
8.10	Over	'Over' is a preposition.
8.11	In	'In' is a preposition.
8.12	Near	'Near' is a preposition.
8.13	Between	'Between' is a preposition.
8.14	Through	'Through' is a preposition.
8.15	On	'On' is a preposition.
8.16	Under	'Under' is a preposition.
8.17	Beside	'Beside' is a preposition.
8.18	Behind	'Behind' is a preposition.

8.19	Near	'Near' is a preposition.
8.20	Above	'Above' is a preposition.
8.21	Under	'Under' is a preposition.
8.22	With	'With' is a preposition.
8.23	Behind	'Behind' is a preposition.
8.24	Inside	'Inside' is a preposition.
8.25	Above	'Above' is a preposition.
8.26	Across	'Across' is a preposition.
8.27	Beside	'Beside' is a preposition.
8.28	Around	'Around' is a preposition.
8.29	Next to	'Next to' is a preposition.
8.30	Among	'Among' is a preposition.
8.31	Next to	'Next to' is a preposition.
8.32	Near	'Near' is a preposition.
8.33	On	'On' is a preposition.
8.34	Beside	'Beside' is a preposition.
8.35	Across	'Across' is a preposition.
8.36	Between	'Between' is a preposition.
8.37	In	'In' is a preposition.
8.38	Underneath	'Underneath' is a preposition.
8.39	Over	'Over' is a preposition.
8.40	Among	'Among' is a preposition.

Ready for More?

The NWEA MAP testing is adaptive. This means that if your student found these questions too tricky or too easy, they may find it useful to practice grades below or above they grade they are in. This will expose students to new concepts and ideas, giving them a better chance at scoring higher in tests.

Alexander-Grace Education produces books covering Mathematics, Sciences, and English, to help your student maximize their potential in these areas.

For errata, please email alexandergraceeducation@gmail.com

ALEXANDER-GRACE EDUCATION

Made in United States
Cleveland, OH
08 April 2025